Indonesia

by Robin Lim

Carolrhoda Books, Inc. / Minneapolis

Photo Acknowledgments

Photographs, maps, and artworks are used courtesy of: John Erste, pp. 1, 2–3, 8–9, 16, 20–21, 24–25, 32–33, 35, 41; Laura Westlund, pp. 4–5, 11, 25 (bottom); © Trip/C.C., pp. 6, 37, 39 (bottom), 40 (left); © Trip/R. Nichols, pp. 7, 27 (top); © Trip/W. Jacobs, p. 8; © Trip/P. Mercea, pp. 9, 13 (right), 40 (right); © Eugene G. Schulz, pp. 10 (left), 20; © Michele Burgess, pp. 10 (right), 12, 14, 16, 17, 18, 26, 30 (top), 33 (left), 36, 38, 43 (left); © Trip/T. Knight, pp. 11, 13 (left); © Trip/A. Tovy, pp. 15 (left), 27 (bottom), 30 (bottom); © Trip/J. Sweeney, p. 15 (right); © Trip/Trip, pp.19, 31 (bottom); © Trip/T. Lester, p. 21 (top); © Trip/D. Clegg, pp. 21 (bottom), 22 (both), 23 (bottom), 32; © Trip/J. Lamb, p. 23 (top); © Betty Crowell, pp. 28, 42; © Trip/J. Pugh, pp. 29, 35; © Trip/T. Bognar, p. 31 (top); © Trip/M. Nichols, p. 33 (right); © Trip/L. Clark, p. 34; © Trip/M. Both, p. 39 (top); © Trip/G. Grieves, p. 43 (right); © Trip/J. Wakelin, p. 44.

Cover photograph of Lombok boys with a string of locusts courtesy of ©Trip/D. Clegg.

Carolrhoda Books, Inc.
A division of Lerner Publishing Group
241 First Avenue North
Minneapolis, MN 55401 U.S.A.

Website address: www.lernerbooks.com

Words in **bold type** are explained in a glossary that begins on page 44.

Library of Congress Cataloging-in-Publication Data

Lim, Robin, 1956–
  Indonesia / Robin Lim
    p.   cm.—(A ticket to)
  Summary: Examines Indonesia's diverse culture, landscape, and climate.
  ISBN 1-57505-175-3 (lib. bdg. : alk. paper)
  1. Indonesia—Juvenile literature. [1. Indonesia.] I. Title. II. Series.
DS615. L54   2001b
959.8—dc21   00-008586

Manufactured in the United States of America
2 3 4 5 6 7 – JR – 07 06 05 04 03 02

Contents

ASIA

Welcome!

Find Indonesia on the map. Indonesia is made up of more than 13,000 **islands.** The islands pop out of the waters separating

SULU SEA

SUMATRA

MALAYSIA

CELEBES SEA

Barisan Mtns.

KALIMANTAN (BORNEO)

N

SULAWESI (CELEBES)

JAVA SEA

Jakarta

MADURA

Miles

0   100   200   300

0   200   400

Kilometers

JAVA

BALI SEA

FLORES

FLORES

BALI   KOMODO

INDIAN   OCEAN

Australia and the **continent** of Asia. Twelve oceans and seas touch the islands. The Pacific Ocean lies to the northeast of Indonesia. The Indian Ocean is to the south. In the southeast, the Arafura Sea and the Timor Sea separate Indonesia from Australia. The Celebes Sea and the Sulu Sea separate Indonesia from the Philippines in the north.

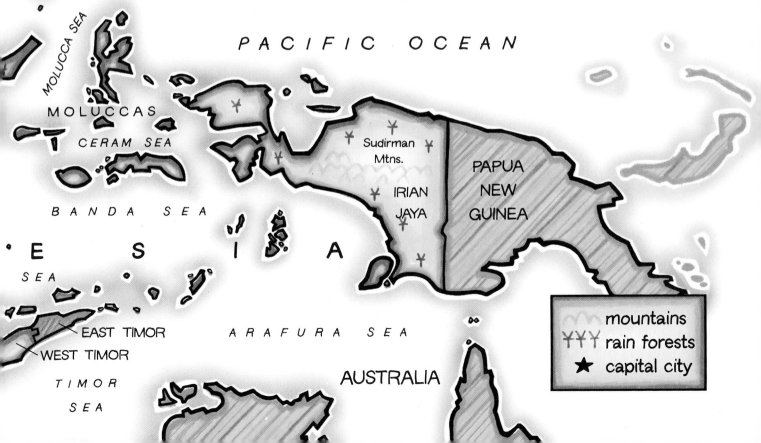

PHILIPPINES

PACIFIC OCEAN

MOLUCCA SEA

MOLUCCAS

CERAM SEA

BANDA SEA

Sudirman Mtns.

IRIAN JAYA

PAPUA NEW GUINEA

E   S   I   A

SEA

EAST TIMOR

WEST TIMOR

ARAFURA SEA

TIMOR SEA

AUSTRALIA

〜〜 mountains
⅄⅄⅄ rain forests
★ capital city

The islands of Indonesia have lots of lush farmland. Rice is the main crop.

Lots of Islands

The big islands of Indonesia are Sumatra, Java, West Timor, Flores, Bali, Celebes, Borneo, and half of New Guinea.

Sumatra is dotted with forests, swamps, and mountains. The island of Java is where most Indonesians (the people of Indonesia) live. It is home to Jakarta, the nation's capital. In Bali **volcanoes** spike the land in the north.

A big **plain** covers the middle of the island. Tiny Flores has 14 volcanoes.

It is easy to get lost in a tropical rain forest. The trees grow so thick they block out the sun.

Map Whiz Quiz

Take a look at the map on pages 4 and 5. Trace the outline of Indonesia onto a piece of paper. Use a green crayon to color the islands. Can you find the Celebes Sea? Mark it with an "N" for north. Look for the Timor Sea. Mark it with an "S" for south. Use a blue crayon to color the seas and oceans around the islands.

Earthquake!

The islands of Indonesia have a lot of **earthquakes.** During an earthquake, parts of the earth shift and cause the ground to move. Some earthquakes cause lots of damage.

Many of the islands were once volcanoes. Indonesia has more than 125 volcanoes that still **erupt.** When

Volcanic ash enriches the soil, helping crops grow tall and strong.

8

Ring of Fire

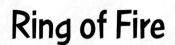

Use your finger to trace a circle on a globe. Start in Indonesia and move north through the Philippines and Japan. Then head east to touch the Russian Federation and Alaska. Run your finger south along the coasts of North and South America. Sweep over to New Zealand to the east, then return to Indonesia. This is called the Ring of Fire. Most of the world's earthquakes and volcanoes happen here.

this happens, hot melted rock pours from the top of the volcano.

Pick up a bunch of tropical flowers at the market in Jakarta (above). *You can visit Sumatran tigers in the zoo* (below right).

arnoldi is the world's biggest flower. It grows on the island of Sumatra. Sumatra is also home to lots of animals, including rhinoceroses, orangutans, Sumatran tigers, tapirs, and elephants.

Big Wildlife

Thousands of plants cover the Indonesian islands. The rafflesia

Dear Grandpa,

Yesterday we took a ferry to the island of Komodo to see the dragons. Wow! Komodo dragons have scales like a fish. They can grow to be more than 12 feet long. The dragons use their tongues to smell. Komodo dragons have more than 60 teeth. And boy, are they sharp! I wanted to take a dragon home, but Mom said, "No way."

Selamat jalan! (That's "happy travels" in Bahasa Indonesia, the official language of Indonesia.)

—Josh

Sun Maintian
Waum Kaillian
Thaluuhu, Simlu
Lamatten

Komodo dragons are really just huge lizards.

The Queen Alexandra's Birdwing is the world's largest butterfly. From the tip of one wing to the tip of the other is 11 inches. That is as long as your arm!

Indonesia's hot weather is great for growing rice in fields called sawahs.

First People

The Malay people arrived in Indonesia 4,000 years ago. No people had lived there before. The Malay built wooden houses on the coasts. They wove cloth and made pottery bowls. They grew rice to eat. More Malay people arrived in Indonesia almost 2,000 years later. This group ate rice and other plants.

Weavers (below) *and potters* (right) *still make colorful cloth and bowls just like Indonesians did long ago.*

Java Man

More than 100 years ago, Eugene Dubois dug up a skull in central Java. It belonged to Java Man, an early relative of humans. Java Man lived 500,000 years ago. Since then, scientists have found bones in Indonesia that are even older than Java Man.

People Mix

Indonesia has about 300 different **ethnic groups,** including the Javanese, Sundanese, and Madurese. Many of Indonesia's political leaders are Javanese. The Sundanese farm rice in west Java. Many Madurese live in east Java. The Madurese are from Madura, an island northeast of Java.

Different kinds of people live in Indonesia. This man and his daughter are Sundanese.

On Sumatra, the Kubu live along the eastern coast. The Batak grow rice in the valleys of northern Sumatra.

Do you wear cartoon T-shirts like these kids (top left) *from Bali? The girls above are Yali. Their relatives came from Australia.*

Northern Folks

In the northern part of Indonesia are the islands of Kalimantan, Sulawesi, the Moluccas, and Irian Jaya. The Malay-Indonesian people live along the coasts in

A ricing hat keeps this Torajan girl cool when she works in the fields.

From the Stars

Toraja means "the people from above." At night the Toraja often point out a group of stars. They believe they came from those stars long ago.

Kalimantan. The Toraja call the mountains on Sulawesi home. Long ago the Toraja sailed to Indonesia from Cambodia. Some Papuans farm in the high valleys and **plateaus** of Irian Jaya. Pygmy people live in the mountains of Irian Jaya.

Dayak women (above) wear golden rings that stretch their earlobes down. This has been a Dayak custom for many years.

Family

In Indonesia's small villages, lots of kids live in houses with their parents, brothers, sisters, grandparents, aunts, uncles, and cousins. All the grown-ups take turns looking after the young ones. Family life is different in the cities. Kids live with their parents, brothers, sisters, and sometimes a grandparent.

A traditional house in Indonesia is shaped like a boat (left). *It's big enough for lots of family members. In cities, kids usually share a house with their parents only* (facing page).

Family Members

Here are some Bahasa Indonesia words for family members.

grandfather	*kakek*	kah-KEHK
grandmother	*nenek*	neh-NEHK
father	*ayah*	EYE-yah
mother	*ibu*	EE-boo
uncle	*paman*	pah-MAHN
aunt	*bibi*	BEE-bee
son	*anak lalaki*	AH-nahk lah-lah-KEE
daughter	*anak prempuan*	AH-nahk prehm-PWAHN
younger sibling	*adik*	AH-dihk
older sibling	*kakak*	kah-KAHK

Zoom around the big city of Jakarta in a three-wheeled taxi!

Indonesia's cities are crowded and noisy. Watch out when you cross the road! Taxis, cars, buses, horse-drawn carriages, and people fill the streets. On *speda motors* (motorbikes), people may carry dozens of eggs or even couches and chairs.

In Jakarta new office buildings, department stores, and hotels tower. Most families live in concrete houses with tile

Streets in Jakarta are jam-packed with cars, taxis, and buses (left). In the countryside, the roads are almost empty (below).

roofs. Some poor folks live in tiny wood and cardboard houses with tin roofs.

21

Country Living

(Left) *Would you like to get a ride from a water buffalo? A young Indonesian wears a bit of his family's rice harvest* (above).

What kinds of chores do you have to do at home? Kids who live in the Indonesian countryside help make grass roofs for their homes.

Kids in the country feed pigs and pluck chickens.

On Indonesian farms, kids help protect the growing rice from hungry birds.

Farmers build rice fields that look like steps into the hillside (above). *After harvesting the rice, farmers separate the seeds from the plants by hand* (below).

Families make scarecrows to trick the creatures. Kids run through the rice fields to shoo away the birds. The kids yell and wave their arms.

Speak Up!

In Indonesia, people use more than 365 languages. Most Indonesians can speak two or more languages. At home kids speak the language their parents grew up speaking. At school Indonesian kids learn Bahasa Indonesia, the nation's official language. Bahasa is based on the Malay and Javanese languages. When they get older, some kids learn English.

Selamat siang

Greet an Indonesian

Here are a few greetings in Bahasa Indonesia. Try them out on a friend!

blessings on your morning	*selamat pagi*	she-lah-MAHT PAH-gee
blessings on your midday	*selamat siang*	she-lah-MAHT see-AHNG
blessings on your late day	*selamat sore*	she-lah-MAHT soh-RAY
blessings on your night	*selamat malam*	she-lah-MAHT mah-LAHM
blessings on your sleep	*selamat tidur*	she-lah-MAHT tee-DOR
sweet dreams	*mimpi manis*	MIHM-pee MAH-nees

On the Indonesian flag, red means courage and white means purity.

25

Religion

Most Indonesians are Muslims (people who practice Islam). In the major cities, you might hear the call to prayer over a crackly loudspeaker. People stop what they are doing. They kneel on the ground. They pray facing west, toward the holy city of Mecca, in Saudi Arabia.

Some Indonesians believe that all

Muslims worship at mosques like this one on Sumatra Island.

natural things—
including plants,
animals, and rocks—
have a spirit. Some
Indonesians may
blend this belief with
another religion.

Hindu temples are packed with visitors when the weather is warm (above). You can have a picnic under the umbrellas at this Hindu temple on Bali Island (left).

27

Ramadan

Ramadan is the holiest time of year in Islam. For Ramadan, the ninth month of the year, adult Muslims do not eat or drink all day. This is called fasting.

Indonesian Muslim families get up before dawn. They eat and drink as much as they can. At sunrise

Muslim women cover their heads with scarves.

Muslim kindergartners get a snack break.

Muslim villagers pray together. All eating and drinking stops for the day. Muslims pray again at sunset. After they pray, everyone can eat.

After Ramadan

The three days after Ramadan are called id al-Fitr. Families visit and share special sweet treats and dates. People ask each other for forgiveness for the wrongs they have done.

During recess, kids might play soccer (left) *or another game. Students wear uniforms for gym class* (below).

Going to School

In Indonesia kids get to school before the teachers. They sweep the playground. Some water plants and trees in the school's garden.

Grades one through six are called Sekola Dasar, or SD. Students study math, reading, writing, history, government, religion, and

Hari Raya Saraswati

Balinese children and teachers celebrate Hari Raya Saraswati. Saraswati is the Hindu goddess of learning. On Saraswati's day, no one reads books, plays instruments, or uses computers. Kids get the day off from school. They put on their nicest sarongs. They pray together in the schoolyard. The smell of **incense** fills the air.

On Saraswati's day, women carry baskets of fruit to offer to the goddess.

social studies. In citizenship class, kids learn how to work together.

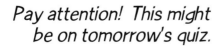

Pay attention! This might be on tomorrow's quiz.

31

Wear a Sarong

Have you ever worn a sarong? A sarong is a six-foot-long piece of cloth that people wrap around the waist and tie. In Indonesia lots of people wear sarongs.

Indonesian boys and girls wear sarongs. Wrap a sheet around your waist and see how comfortable it is!

To make a sarong, weavers weave a thick cotton called ikat. Weavers use brown, deep red, and dark blue thread to weave designs into the cloth.

Artists use hot wax and dye to make cool designs on cloth. This is called batik (left). Dark ikat cloth is used for sarongs and traditional clothing (below).

Pictures of birds, roses, and angels are popular.

33

Puppet Show

In Indonesian cities, you can buy a puppet on the street.

Late at night on the islands of Java and Bali, people gather to watch *wayang kulit* (shadow puppets). A white screen hides the *dalang* **(puppeteer)** from the audience. The dalang moves the puppets to show a favorite **folktale.** The show lasts all night.

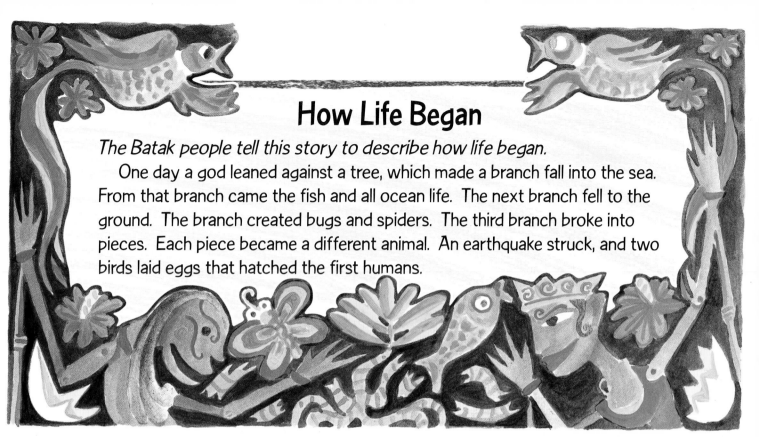

How Life Began

The Batak people tell this story to describe how life began.

One day a god leaned against a tree, which made a branch fall into the sea. From that branch came the fish and all ocean life. The next branch fell to the ground. The branch created bugs and spiders. The third branch broke into pieces. Each piece became a different animal. An earthquake struck, and two birds laid eggs that hatched the first humans.

Puppets come in all sizes and colors.

Bamboo Music

Bamboo trees grow all over Indonesia. Musicians use bamboo to make instruments. Schoolchildren of the Moluccas carry their bamboo flutes with them wherever they go.

Kids can join a band and play music with bamboo flutes.

Indonesians keep dancing alive with traditional movements and costumes.

In the Moluccas, two long bamboo poles are used in the *bambu gila* or "dangerous dance." Two dancers kneel and click the poles together in time to the music. Other dancers step and jump between the poles as the music gets faster and faster.

After they make sure each piece is perfect, wood carvers sell their work at markets.

Young Artists

Art is a big part of Indonesian life. People wear handwoven sarongs. They cook meals in bowls made by a potter. They sit on finely carved wood furniture.

Kids in Indonesia carve, paint, or weave as soon as they are old enough to walk.

Parents expect their children to be skilled crafters by about age 12.

Some Indonesians make baskets from grasses (top right). *Long ago, people carved these statues* (above) *to remember relatives who had died.*

39

Fast Food

Have you ever tried to walk and eat at the same time? Indonesians who sell food at outdoor markets make food easy to carry, such as roasted chicken on a stick.

Tutti Frutti

The fruit in Indonesia is really tasty. There are mangoes, bananas, pineapples, coconuts, and papayas. Try the hairy *red rambutan*, the snake-skinned *salak*, or the honey-flavored *sawo*.

Hungry? Look for vendors pushing little carts. They sell *bakso, satay* (roasted chicken on a stick), or *gado-gado.* Bakso is a steaming bowl of soup filled with vegetables, noodles, and little balls of meat. Gado-gado is vegetables and rice topped with a tasty peanut sauce. For

Carrots, celery, potatoes, and broccoli are the main ingredients in gado-gado.

dessert try *janjan.* Cooks make janjan with rice flour and raw sugar from the coconut palm.

Ocean breezes easily lift kites into the air.

Fly a Kite

What's that in the sky? You might see kites shaped like birds, bats, boxes, rocket ships, or butterflies. Kite festivals are big in the month of March. Most Indonesian kids like to make their own kites. Kids join clubs to build really big kites.

Soccer is the number-one sport in Indonesia. Kids play whenever they can—during recess and after school. Watching a cock fight—two roosters fighting each other—is an entertaining way to spend an afternoon in Indonesia. Stay behind the fence, though!

On the day of the festival, kids carry the huge kites to the beach. Ocean winds send the kites high in the air.

Everyone join hands! These kids from the countryside dance during a celebration.

New Words to Learn

continent: Any one of seven large areas of land. A few of the continents are Africa, Asia, and North America.

earthquake: A shaking of the ground caused by the shifting of underground rock.

erupt: To throw forth melted rock, ash, and smoke.

ethnic group: A group of people with many things in common, such as language, religion, and customs.

44

folktale: A timeless story told by word of mouth from grandparent to parent to child. Many folktales have been written down in books.

incense: Thin wood sticks coated in spices that give off a sweet smell when burned.

island: A piece of land surrounded by water.

plain: A broad, flat area of land that has few trees or other outstanding natural features.

plateau: A large area of high, level land.

puppeteer: A person who stands behind a stage and makes a puppet move by pulling the puppet's strings.

volcano: An opening in the earth's surface through which hot, melted rock shoots up. *Volcano* can also mean the hill or mountain of ash and rock that builds up around the opening.

New Words to Say

Bahasa	bah-wah-SAH
bakso	BAHK-soh
Bali	BAH-lee
bambu gila	BAHM-boo GEE-lah
Celebes	sehl-AH-beez
dalang	dah-LAHNG
gado-gado	GAH-doh GAH-doh
Hari Raya Saraswati	HAH-ree RAH-yah sah-rah-SWAH-tee
id al-Fitr	EED AHL FEE-tree
ikat	EE-kaht
Indonesia	ihn-doh-NEE-zhah
janjan	JAH-jahn
Komodo	kah-MOH-doh
Pygmy	PIHG-mee
rafflesia arnoldi	rah-fleh-SEE-ah ahr-NOHL-dee
sarong	sah-RONG
satay	SAH-tay
sawahs	SAH-wahz
Sekola Dasar	seh-KOH-lah DAH-sahr
Sumatra	Soo-MAH-trah
wayang kulit	wah-YANG koo-LEET

More Books to Read

Clarke, Penny. *Volcanoes.* Danbury, CT: Franklin Watts, 1998.

Cox, David. *Ayu and the Perfect Moon.* London: The Bodley Head, 1984.

Kimishima, Hisako. *The Princess of the Rice Fields: An Indonesian Folktale.* New York: Walker/Weatherhill, 1970.

Maynard, Thane. *Komodo Dragons.* Chanhassen, MN: The Child's World, Inc., 1997.

Ryan, Patrick. *Indonesia.* Chanhassen, MN: The Child's World, Inc., 1998.

Simon, Seymour. *Earthquakes.* New York: Morrow Junior Books, 1991.

New Words to Find